SPOONBILL. Large wings, steady beat. Head and neck extended. Long legs stretched out behind.

DIVERS. Thickish neck stretched out with head lowered. Small wings, fast wing-beat. Legs extended.

AVOCET. Head and neck partly extended. Legs extend well beyond tail. Rapid wing-beat.

DUCKS. Very fast. Pointed wings, rapid wing-beat. Head and neck extended, feet tucked under tail.

SWANS. Very long neck extended. Large wing with slow steady wing-beat. Wings make throbbing sound.

RAILS. Neck extended, legs often dangling. Weak flight, small wings; usually short distances only.

GREBES. Thin neck extended, head and tail low. 'Hump-backed' look. Legs trailing behind. Small wings.

HERONS & BITTERNS. Head and neck retracted, legs stretched out behind. Slow wing-beat on large wings.

A Ladybird Nature Book
Series 536

Although — for brevity — the title of this book is 'Pond and River Birds', it also includes some which frequent small streams, lochs, lakes and reservoirs, and even areas near the sea.

As with the other bird books in this series, superb illustrations have been specially prepared by John Leigh-Pemberton.

POND and RIVER BIRDS

by
JOHN LEIGH-PEMBERTON

Publishers: Ladybird Books Ltd . Loughborough
© Ladybird Books Ltd (formerly Wills & Hepworth Ltd) 1969
Printed in England

Bittern *(above)*
Spotted Crake *(below)*

Both these uncommon birds are inhabitants of reed-beds and swamps, and are more often heard than seen. They are most active at twilight and spend much of the day hiding in thick cover.

The Bittern has gradually increased in numbers after having become extinct in this country at the end of the last century. Since 1911, however, it has bred here again, chiefly in East Anglia. The nest, built of reeds and grass, is placed among reed-stems as near as possible to shallow water. Four to six eggs are laid. Nest-building, tending and feeding the young, are performed by the hen alone. Food consists of fish, frogs, small mammals and some vegetation. The Bittern's most notable feature is the spring-time call of the male—a deep, resounding 'boom' which is audible three miles away.

Unlike the resident Bittern, the Spotted Crake is a summer visitor which only occasionally winters here but has bred fairly often. It has become a rare bird in many of its former haunts, owing to the drainage of marshes and fens. In this country it occurs chiefly in Somerset, its presence being most often revealed by the characteristic cry, said to be similar to the crack of a whip—'hwip'—or to the loud ticking of a clock.

The neat little nest, placed in thick grass, contains as many as twelve eggs, and two broods are raised by both parents. Its food is varied, consisting of snails and flies as well as some seeds and water plants.

4

7214 0112 0

Heron

The Heron is a resident, one of the largest birds we have. Although quite common, its numbers seem to vary, especially after a hard winter. It is found in any watery locality, from the sea-shore to mountain streams, but it usually nests in a colony—called a 'heronry'—in high trees. The nests themselves are structures of sticks which, used year after year, become larger and larger as repairs and additions take place. The nest is lined with grass and from three to five greenish-blue eggs are laid, often as early as February. Incubation and care of the young is by both parents, and sometimes there are two broods.

The Heron is a great fisherman—standing solitary and motionless in the shallows until suddenly the neck and powerful bill are shot out to seize the prey. This consists chiefly of fish and eels, but mammals such as rats, water voles and even rabbits are also taken.

In spite of their size and considerable wing span, Herons weigh only about three and a half to four pounds. This lightness in relation to the wing area enables the Heron to rise remarkably quickly and to soar with ease to considerable heights. In flight the head is drawn back upon the shoulders and the legs are stretched out behind. The usual cry is a harsh 'frank', usually uttered in flight, but many other cries and sounds are used, especially near the nest.

Reed Bunting *(above: hen left, cock right)*

Willow Tit *(below: left)*

Marsh Tit *(below: right)*

The fringes of areas of water have their own species of small birds which depend for their food on water insects and the seeds of water plants. One such is the handsome Reed Bunting, a resident bird which nests among reed beds but usually spends the winter on farm land. Our Reed Bunting population is constantly changing, some birds emigrating while others come here from Europe. In spring, returning migrant cocks arrive before the hens.

The nest, which sometimes contains the flowers of reeds, is either on the ground or in a tree stump, and four or five eggs are laid. As many as three broods are raised by both parents. The song varies, but consists chiefly of an often repeated 'twee-tititick'.

Both Marsh and Willow Tits can be found in woodland or marshy ground and both of them like to nest in holes in such trees as alders or willows. They are very alike, the best way of telling them apart being by the song; the Marsh Tit has a typical 'pitchiu-u' call, while the Willow Tit has a warbling song, quite unlike that of any other tit, and a characteristic deep 'zurr-zurr'. The Willow Tit has a light wing patch and a dull black head. The head of the Marsh Tit tends to be glossy. The nests are somewhat alike, both being built upon a thick pad of hair and moss. Willow Tits lay eight or nine eggs, Marsh Tits usually fewer.

Kingfisher *(above)*
Dipper *(below)*

The Kingfisher is a resident, found on slow-moving rivers and streams throughout England, Wales and the lowlands of Scotland. In winter it is sometimes seen on the sea coast.

The food of the Kingfisher consists almost entirely of small fish, although insects and tadpoles are also eaten. It fishes by perching on a branch overhanging the water, from which it darts and picks its prey from the stream. Sometimes it hovers like a hawk, but its normal flight is fast and low over the water. The cry, usually uttered in flight, is a loud, harsh 'chi-kee' and the song is made up of a series of whistles.

Kingfishers nest in burrows which they bore to a depth of about three feet into a river bank. Six or seven eggs are laid and fish bones are placed round these during the incubation period. There are two broods.

The Dipper is another resident, not found in eastern or southern England, and favours fast-running streams. It bobs restlessly up and down, plunging into the water in search of the small fish and water insects on which it feeds. It can walk about under water and is a good swimmer and rapid flyer. Five eggs are laid in a nest which is lined with leaves and has a sort of roof over it. Usually there are two broods. The song is a rippling warble, uttered by both sexes, and the usual cry is a loud 'zit-zit'.

Bearded Tit *(above: hen left, cock right)*

Sedge Warbler *(below: left)*

Reed Warbler *(below: right)*

The Bearded Tit lives only among reeds, climbing acrobatically up and down the stems or flying with rapid, whirring wing beats just above them. This is a resident in Norfolk and Suffolk, although twenty years ago it was almost extinct. It nests among reeds, just above ground level, and lays from five to seven eggs in a nest built of dead reeds and lined with reed flowers and feathers. Reed seeds are the main item of diet, although caterpillars and water flies are also taken. There is no song, but the vibrating call-note, 'ping-ping', is distinctive.

Many small Warblers, summer visitors, favour the protection of reed beds, finding there the insects upon which they mainly feed. The Sedge Warbler, distinguished by its eye-stripe, is generally distributed in suitable parts of Britain. From April to July it delivers a very varied song, part melodious, part grating. The nest is large, placed low down in thick cover, built of grass and stalks and lined with hair and feathers. Five or six eggs, sometimes in two broods, are raised by both cock and hen. Like most small warblers, its flight is low and for short distances only.

The Reed Warbler hides in the cover of reeds, where it builds a large, cylindrical nest which is often attached to the reed stems and is lined most elaborately with a great variety of soft materials. Only four or five eggs are laid and incubation and tending the young are by both parents.

Coot (above)

Moorhen (below)

These two well-known birds belong to the Rail family, which in Britain includes also the Crakes and Water Rails. The feet of all of them are to some extent provided with pads or 'lobes'. All tend to hide in vegetation at the edges of fresh-water areas. They are poor flyers but swim, dive and run well.

The Coot is a resident which breeds throughout Britain, preferring lakes or reservoirs to the smaller ponds or slow-moving streams favoured by the Moorhen. Its food is chiefly vegetable matter such as water weed, for which it dives, but it will also eat fish and worms. The Coot lays six to nine eggs (although there can be as many as fifteen) in a large nest almost at water level, but built above it with dead reeds. There are at least two broods, and three days after hatching, the young leave the nest. The Coot's cry is a loud 'kwok'.

The smaller Moorhen's cry is either a croak or a sharp 'kittick'. Like the Coot, this bird has some difficulty in taking flight, and both patter along the surface for some distance before becoming airborne. Moorhens' food is more varied than that of Coots, and they will more readily nest on land. As many as ten eggs are laid and there are two or three broods, the young of early broods helping to tend the later families. This is a bolder bird than the other Rails, and is quite common in town parks.

Little Grebe *(above)*
Water Rail *(below)*

The Little Grebe or Dabchick is the smallest and commonest of the British Grebes, of which there are five species. Grebes are diving birds, able to stay submerged for up to thirty seconds and at depths of about twenty feet. They have more feathers than other birds and their feet are fringed with 'lobes'.

The Little Grebe, a resident, is generally distributed in water areas varying from lakes to small ponds. Four to six eggs are laid in a nest made of rushes and which is heaped up above the water under overhanging vegetation. There are two broods and the young are raised by both parents, who sometimes carry them on their backs. Food consists of fish, insects and some vegetable matter. The cry is oddly like the shrill whinnying of a horse.

The Water Rail is more likely to be heard than seen, for it is a shy bird which hides among reed beds or thick vegetation. It is a resident whose numbers are reinforced in winter by immigrant birds, and it is commonest in Norfolk and in Ireland. The cries, all of them very unmusical, can vary from a grunt to a scream, or even a purring sound, and this bird is particularly noisy at night. It nests among reeds, but above the water level, and from six to eleven eggs are laid; there are two broods. Food is the same as for other members of the Rail family, and like them it is a weak flyer.

Great Crested Grebe *(above)*
Slavonian Grebe *(below)*

The Great Crested Grebe is one of our most beautiful water birds, and has a very interesting courtship display. A hundred years ago it was almost exterminated owing to the demand for its feathers, but it is now a well established and wide-spread resident. It likes large, shallow areas of water with reeds or bushes for cover. Like all Grebes, it has practically no tail, and its small wings make it necessary for it to fly with rapid wing-beats. The nest is built of weeds and some sticks, just above the water level, and is anchored to reeds or bushes. Three or four eggs are laid and the young are carried on the back of one parent, while the other feeds them. Food consists of fish, insects, newts and some vegetable matter. It utters a sort of bark—'garr'—and there are other cries.

Another resident is the Slavonian Grebe, a smaller bird which breeds on lochs and ponds in parts of Scotland, but which, like the other Grebes, spends the winter at sea in a sheltered bay or estuary. It is bolder than most Grebes and flies more readily. It has a low 'kowee' call, frequently repeated. Food is the same as that of other Grebes, and the nest is similar—a heap of water weeds with a depression in the centre. In this depression are laid three to five eggs, which are covered with vegetable material when the parents leave the nest.

Red-necked Grebe *(above: summer left, winter right)*
Black-necked Grebe *(below)*

Not quite so large as the Great Crested Grebe is the
Red-necked Grebe, which is chiefly a winter visitor to
eastern England and the lowlands of Scotland. It occurs
occasionally at other times of the year, when it may be
seen in its summer plumage. It is a rare bird, seen mostly
on the sea close to the shore, and is very like the Great
Crested Grebe in its habits, and has a very similar,
though higher-pitched cry, 'keek-keek'. Like all other
Grebes, it eats large quantities of its own feathers as
well as the normal diet, and this is believed to help the
digestion. The Red-necked Grebe does not breed in
Britain.

The Black-necked Grebe is considerably smaller and
is a resident in a few localities throughout Britain. It is
nowhere numerous, although at one time there was quite
a large colony in Ireland. Shyer than the Slavonian
Grebe, it is similar in other respects, the food and
nesting habits being the same. Although it swims fairly
high in the water, it can, when agitated, sink its body
until its back is awash—a trick shared with the other
Grebes.

Three or four eggs, sometimes in two broods, are
hatched in about three weeks. At seventeen days old,
young Black-necked Grebes have become expert divers,
but it is a full month before they are independent of
their parents. The cry is a soft 'pip-peep-houeet'.

Great Northern Diver

Divers, sometimes called Loons, are birds of the open water, spending the winter on salt water but coming to lakes and slow-flowing rivers to breed. Unlike most other birds, they have solid bones, and are capable of expelling the air from their bodies and feathers. This makes it possible for them to submerge without any effort, and they will often sink rather than dive when alarmed or feeding. They are strong flyers, but have small wings and, therefore, fly with a rapid wing-beat. Their legs, which have webbed, not 'lobed' feet, are placed so far back in their bodies that they are almost helpless on land. Divers can descend to great depths and, if necessary, stay submerged for several minutes, although the normal dive is for about half a minute only. Fish, crabs, shrimps and worms are the principal items of diet.

The Great Northern Diver does not breed in the British Isles, being a winter visitor chiefly to the northern coasts and to Shetland, where it is present throughout the year. It is a large, silent bird, which flies only reluctantly and, like the grebes, has some difficulty in rising from the water. It also requires a considerable stretch of water on which to land. Under water, however, it is a magnificent performer, its whole shape seeming to be designed for diving and swimming at speed.

The Great Northern Diver breeds in Iceland, Greenland and North America.

Red-throated Diver *(above: winter left, summer right)*
Black-throated Diver *(below)*

The Red-throated Diver is a resident of the Scottish Highlands and Islands, and is found in small numbers in Northern Ireland. Of all the Divers it is the best and strongest flyer, frequently flying quite high and taking off more easily than other Divers from small stretches of water. It is quite a sociable bird and sometimes nests in colonies. Like other Divers, its helplessness on land makes it necessary for it to nest as close to the water as possible. The nest may be on land or in very shallow water, and is either built of wet moss and weeds or consists of nothing more than a hollow pressed out in the grass or heather. Two eggs are laid, and these are incubated for about twenty-eight days by both parents. There is only one brood.

Both the Red-throated and Black-throated Divers have a deep 'kuk-kuk-kuk' cry, used repeatedly in flight.

The Black-throated Diver is also a resident of northern Scotland and the Outer Hebrides. It is not as strong a flyer as the Red-throated Diver, and is more inclined to nest near longer stretches of water, preferring to do so on a small islet. In other respects it is much the same. It is the rarest of the Divers, and the one which seems most to resent interference by man.

In the winter both these birds assume a much less spectacular plumage, mostly grey and white, and spend their time at sea near the coast.

Spoonbill

The Spoonbill is not a very large bird, but appears to be so because of its long bill and neck. It is a regular visitor to East Anglia in both summer and winter, and occasionally to places on the south coast. In the eighteenth century it bred in England and Wales, but it does not now breed here—the nearest breeding colony being in Holland at the mouth of the Rhine, and our visiting birds come from there.

The extraordinary bill is specially adapted to its method of feeding. It wades through the shallow water of the marshes it frequents with its head held low and the broad, flattened tip of its bill dipped in the water. The bill is swept from side to side with a scythe-like action and food is collected. This consists of small fish, crabs, worms and insects and, like most water birds, a certain amount of weed. In flight the Spoonbill is impressive, capable of soaring to a considerable height and flying with neck and legs stretched out. The wing beat is regular and rapid.

Spoonbills occur in parties, and nest in colonies usually in high trees but sometimes in reed beds. The nesting site is rarely far from the coast. In winter they migrate to Africa.

This is a very silent bird—the only sounds coming from it seem to be a series of grunts and sighs when nesting, and a clapping of the bill when angry.

Avocet

The Avocet provides another example of a bird with a bill specially adapted to its feeding method. The Avocet's up-turned bill—itself a rarity among birds—is used for sweeping from side to side in shallow water or in mud. Shrimps, worms and other animal matter is thus collected, and the presence of an Avocet is often indicated by the characteristic marks made in the mud by this sweeping action. The Avocet will also feed while swimming and will 'up-end' (head under water, tail straight up out of it) like a duck.

After being extinct as a breeding species in Britain for many years, the Avocet has once more become established in Suffolk, since 1940, breeding there and in a few other places regularly. It is by no means a common bird, but a most beautiful one to watch, whether wading, swimming or flying, and it should be most carefully protected. Special societies exist for the protection of birds, and it is a good idea to join one.

The Avocet lays four eggs in a hollow on the ground, often quite unlined but sometimes surrounded by a mass of dead vegetation. Both parents incubate and feed the young, and there is one brood. The bill of young Avocets is straight until they are a week old, and they can fly at six weeks.

Salt-marshes, river estuaries or mud-flats are the Avocet's habitat, and it has a clear, fluty 'kluik' cry.

Mute Swan and Cygnets

Swans are large, powerful birds which generally prefer stretches of water sufficiently extensive to enable them to take off or settle without difficulty. At times they are found at sea near the coast, but they nest on land, usually close to water, and often on an island. They are almost entirely vegetarian, feeding on weed which they collect by dipping the head and long neck well under water, or by 'up-ending' like a duck. The male is called a 'cob' and the female a 'pen'.

All swans fly with slow, regular wing beats, carrying the head and neck stretched out.

The Mute Swan was long thought to have been introduced into Britain, but from fossil remains it is now known that it has always been a resident bird. It is at present increasing in numbers, and is found almost throughout Britain. It is aggressive, particularly at breeding time, and will attack other waterfowl and even dogs and humans. It is almost silent but will hiss when angry; in flight, however, the wings make a distinctive throbbing noise on the air which can be heard some way off.

From five to seven pale bluish-green eggs are laid in a large nest, which is really a heap of water vegetation with a central hollow. Both parents incubate, and the young—or cygnets—hatch in thirty-five days. They leave the nest and are able to swim a few days later, and are tended by both cob and pen. There is only one brood.

Bewick's Swan (above)
Whooper Swan (below)

Both these swans have yellow and black bills without 'knobs', in contrast to the Mute Swan which has an orange bill with a black knob (larger in the case of the cob). They do not carry their necks in such a graceful curve and they are much wilder birds than the Mute Swan, which is usually semi-domesticated.

The Whooper Swan is a winter visitor, chiefly to sheltered bays or sea-lochs of northern Scotland and to a few other places in Britain. Occasionally it stays for the summer and has been known to breed. When it does so, the pen builds the nest with material supplied by the cob; this consists of moss, weed and quite a large amount of earth. The five or six eggs are a dirty, yellowish white, and only the pen incubates. There is only one brood.

On the wing the Whooper Swan has a trumpet-like call 'whoo-whoop', from which it gets its name. In flight its wings make a less vibrant noise than those of the Mute Swan.

A slightly smaller, though in many ways similar bird is Bewick's Swan, which has a different pattern of black and yellow on the bill and is generally more goose-like in appearance. It does not breed in Britain, but is a regular winter visitor to the Fen country, to the Severn and to Wales. The cry of Bewick's Swan is a 'kong-hong' call, more like that of a goose*.

*For geese see
'Sea and Estuary Birds'.   32

Mallard *(duck left, drake right)*

Generally speaking, British ducks can be divided into four groups: Shelduck*, surface-feeding ducks, diving ducks and sawbills. Shelduck have much in common with geese and are largely marine in habit. Surface-feeding ducks are found on marshes and ponds, while diving ducks belong to larger stretches of water and to the sea. Sawbills are divers, but have special toothed bills with which they catch fish. Males are 'drakes' and females 'ducks'.

All ducks have webbed feet and all pass through an annual period, after the breeding season, when they lose all their flight feathers simultaneously and are unable to fly. This is the 'eclipse' period, during which the drake assumes a plumage very similar to the duck's.

The Mallard is our commonest duck, a resident throughout Britain on practically every type of water. It is a surface feeder, living almost entirely on water weed but also eating a few frogs, worms and crabs. The nest is usually under cover, sometimes in a hole in a tree, but most often on the ground. From ten to twelve eggs are incubated by the duck, who also builds the nest and lines it with feathers. On hatching, the young are led by the duck to water to which they take at once. Usually there is only one brood.

The flight of the Mallard is very fast, and it can rise almost straight up out of the water. Only the duck makes the well-known 'quack' noise, the drake being much quieter.

Tufted Duck *(above: drakes left, duck right)*

Teal *(below: drake left, duck right)*

The Tufted Duck is a diver which has rapidly increased in numbers during the present century and which has readily adapted to all sorts of habitat including lakes or reservoirs in urban areas. As a diver its food consists of water insects, frogs and small fish. It is a resident, breeding in many suitable areas, though not frequently in Wales or south-eastern England. It nests near the water, under cover, laying as many as fourteen eggs; all incubation and tending of the ducklings are by the duck alone. The drake has a low whistle and the duck a harsh 'carragh' instead of the 'quack' of surface-feeding ducks.

Teal are the smallest of British ducks, surface feeders, resident over most of Britain though most numerous in the east and north. This pretty little bird is an agile and rapid flyer, able to shoot straight up from a small area of water and often occurring in quite large flocks. It feeds mostly at night, its food being the same as that of the other surface feeders.

Teal build nests on dry ground among heather or in woodland among bracken, which is often used by the duck in constructing a nest which is afterwards lined with leaves and down. Incubation of the eight to ten eggs is by the duck alone, but the drake helps in tending the young. There is only one brood.

The cry of the drake is 'kvit-kvit' or a whistling 'pripp-pripp'. The duck has a sharp 'quack' when alarmed.

Pochard (above: duck left, drake right)

Shoveler (below: duck left, drake right)

The Pochard is another diving duck, a resident chiefly in the eastern and southern counties of England and in Scotland. It breeds in a few suitable localities and, unlike many ducks, prefers to build a nest on or very close to the water. The nest, a heap of dead vegetation, contains from six to eleven eggs, and there is one brood only. The drake takes no part in incubation or tending the ducklings. Like most diving ducks, its take-off from water is poor and it has to 'patter' across the surface for some distance before becoming airborne.

The Pochard is more vegetarian than most divers, and is a somewhat silent bird except for an alarm call, 'kurr'.

The Shoveler's huge spoon-shaped bill is its outstanding feature. This is specially adapted to feeding on the surface in the very shallow water this species prefers. This duck is a resident, found mostly in the lowlands of Scotland and in northern England but occurring locally elsewhere. In winter, migrating Shovelers arrive from the Continent.

Shovelers, although they look awkward, are almost as agile as Teal in rising from the water, but they are very ungainly on land. They are more silent than most ducks —the drake has a deep 'chock-chock' and the duck a rather feeble 'quack'. The nest is on dry ground, lined with grass and feathers, and eight to twelve eggs are laid. These are hatched and the ducklings tended by the duck alone. There is only one brood.

Scaup *(above: duck left, drake right)*

Pintail *(below: duck left, drake right)*

The Scaup is a diving duck, found chiefly at sea but occasionally coming to Scottish lochs to breed. It is principally a winter visitor to northern coasts and is rare inland. Scaup are tough little birds able to stand cold and rough weather at sea, where they congregate in large flocks. They dive exceptionally deeply and are largely nocturnal feeders. The nest is on the ground and usually protected by heather or grass. Six to eleven eggs in one brood are raised mostly by the duck, who is said to be particularly reluctant to leave her eggs. The Scaup is silent, except for the usual 'karr' of the duck and the soft courting whistles of the drake.

The Pintail, a surface feeder, is probably more numerous than any duck species in the world, being found throughout Europe and in North America, Asia and Africa. It is unusually graceful both on the water and on land, and its flight is very rapid. This shy bird is not a very common resident, being found mostly on coasts of Scotland and East Anglia, with some recent increase in southern England. Its numbers are increased in winter by migrants from Europe.

Pintail nest among grass or heather, preferably on an island, laying seven to nine eggs in a somewhat exposed nest. In common with other ducks, the drake takes little part in incubation or care of the ducklings.

The cry of the Pintail is very rarely heard, but the drake has a soft double whistle.

Long-tailed Duck *(above: drake left, duck right)*
Common Scoter *(below: drake left, duck right)*

The Long-tailed Duck is chiefly a marine species, only coming to land to breed. It is a diver, a winter visitor mostly to the Orkneys (where is has bred) and to Shetland, although it does occur in small numbers elsewhere. The drake is unusual in that, in addition to his eclipse period, he has distinct summer and winter plumages. He is also extremely noisy, his loud cry 'ow-ow-kaloo-kaloo' being used by day and night, both in flight and at rest on the water.

This bird is one of the fastest flyers of all ducks, and has an unusual wing action, the wings dipping well below the body. Flight is low to the water, swinging from side to side. Nesting habits are the same as for other diving ducks, and a single clutch of six to eight eggs is laid among rocks or heather.

The Common Scoter is another marine diving duck and comes to northern Scottish lochs to breed. Elsewhere it is a common visitor in both summer and winter to the coasts of Britain. Rather a heavy bird, it rises from the water with difficulty and usually flies low over it.

The drake has a soft call 'peu-peu-peu' and the duck the usual harsh 'karr'. Like similar species, it nests among heather and lays five to seven eggs, the family being raised entirely by the duck. It is said to be inedible and therefore is not persecuted as are many waterfowl.

Garganey (above: drake left, duck right)

Gadwall (below: drake left, duck right)

Garganey and Gadwall are both surface-feeding ducks, the former somewhat like the Teal and the latter like a small Mallard. Neither is common, but both breed here although only the Gadwall is resident, the little Garganey being a summer visitor.

The Gadwall is a shy bird which nests in thick cover, rather closer to water than most ducks. The duck lines her grassy nest with down from her own breast, as most ducks do, and incubates eight to twelve eggs. There is only one brood. The 'quack' of the duck is very like that of Mallard, and the drake utters a deep 'ep-ep', particularly during courtship. Gadwall are found in stretches of water which have plenty of cover, mostly in East Anglia and at Loch Leven in Scotland, and a few other places.

The Garganey is rare in Wales and Scotland, but breeds regularly in small numbers in some eastern and southern counties of England. It arrives here in March or April, and leaves in August to winter in tropical Africa. It favours the same types of water as Teal, with which it mixes.

The nest is usually in long grass, well hidden and lined with white-tipped down. The duck alone hatches ten or eleven eggs and tends the ducklings. There is only one brood.

The duck has the usual 'quack', but the drake makes the most curious scratching or rattling noise—'klerrep'. Food includes more animal matter than the diet of other surface feeders.

Wigeon *(drake left, duck right)*

Surface feeding ducks all have a bar of bright metallic-coloured feathers on the hind edge of the inner wing. This is called the 'speculum' and, as it varies with each species (and sometimes even between duck and drake of the same species), it is a useful guide to assist identification. The speculum of diving ducks, if it is present, is usually nothing more than a patch of pale feathers.

The Wigeon is a resident in northern Scotland, and to a lesser degree in north-eastern England. Elsewhere in Britain it is a winter visitor from northern Europe. This pretty surface feeder nests on moorland among heather, often close to mountain streams, laying seven or eight eggs in a nest made of bracken and heather and lined, as usual, with down. Nesting and feeding habits are similar to those of other surface-feeding ducks. The bill of the duck is particularly small.

The Wigeon's flight is fast and its take-off from water almost vertical; it is also more at home on land than most ducks. It collects in flocks, especially outside the breeding season when it frequents the sea coast and river estuaries. Flocks fly in tight formation.

The call of the drake is a loud, musical whistling—'whee-you-whee-you', very distinctive and uttered with a fully open beak; there is also a short 'whip-whip' uttered in flight. The duck's alarm note is 'krak-krak', and she also utters a purring note, sometimes in chorus.

Golden-eye *(above: drake left, duck right)*

Smew *(below: drake left, duck right)*

Golden-eye, diving ducks of northern Europe, have only rarely bred here and come to us as winter visitors, chiefly to coasts but sometimes to inland waters. When nesting it builds in a hollow tree or in a rabbit burrow, favouring forest areas; but outside the breeding season it is mostly found at sea or on a river estuary. It is a tough little bird and, unlike most diving ducks, is able to rise quickly from the water. It has a distinctive flight in which the wings produce a rattling whistle; otherwise it is a somewhat silent bird, except for the duck's 'kraah' and the usual odd sounds of courtship display.

The Smew is the smallest representative of the group of ducks known as sawbills. They are given this name on account of the toothed edges of their bills, which are more slender than those of other ducks and are specially adapted for catching and holding fish.

This handsome bird is a winter visitor in small numbers to reservoirs in south-east England, particularly near London. When alarmed it leaps almost vertically into the air, or else sinks its body deep into the water. It is a very rapid flyer and can stay submerged for almost a minute. Like the other Sawbills, it has a crest of feathers on the head which is raised when the bird is agitated.

The Smew has never nested here; like the Golden-eye it likes to nest in forests. It is an almost silent bird.

Goosander *(drake above, duck below)*

Like the Red-breasted Merganser*,the Goosander is a Sawbill duck resident in Scotland, and a winter visitor to inland waters in other parts of Britain. Visiting Mergansers are found in coastal regions, but the Goosander is more strictly an inland bird, favouring particularly the reservoirs in the Thames valley.

The flight of both birds is very fast, low over the water and in a slightly hump-backed attitude. Goosanders are superb divers, able to swim considerable distances under water. They are generally rather silent, except for the duck's call 'karr' and a sort of growl from the drake.

As with other Sawbills, the diet is mainly of fish, but some other animal food is taken. Goosanders like to nest within reach of their fishing area, but in a hollow tree or rock cavity. All incubation and rearing of the young are by the duck, and during this period the drakes form into small flocks. From seven to fourteen or more eggs are laid. These large clutches are typical of the duck family, whose young fall victim to a great many predators. Rats, pike, crows and other water fowl are particularly dangerous to ducklings, and the large family is nature's way of counteracting the losses.

Goosanders, like other Sawbills, have a crest on the back of the head and neck, but with this species it is more evident in the duck than in the drake. In the eclipse period of three to four months, the drake resembles the duck.

* See 'Sea and Estuary Birds' and also for Eider and Shelduck.

INDEX